TRUMPET
101 JAZZ SONGS

ISBN 978-1-4950-2341-5

Hal•Leonard®
CORPORATION
7777 W. BLUEMOUND RD. P.O. BOX 13819 MILWAUKEE, WI 53213

CONTENTS

ALL OF ME

TRUMPET

Words and Music by SEYMOUR SIMONS
and GERALD MARKS

All the Things You Are

TRUMPET

Lyrics by OSCAR HAMMERSTEIN II
Music by JEROME KERN

APRIL IN PARIS

TRUMPET

Words by E.Y. "YIP" HARBURG
Music by VERNON DUKE

AUTUMN IN NEW YORK

TRUMPET

Words and Music by
VERNON DUKE

AUTUMN LEAVES

TRUMPET

English Lyric by JOHNNY MERCER
French Lyric by JACQUES PREVERT
Music by JOSEPH KOSMA

BEWITCHED

TRUMPET

Words by LORENZ HART
Music by RICHARD RODGERS

BEYOND THE SEA

Lyrics by JACK LAWRENCE
Music by CHARLES TRENET and ALBERT LASRY
Original French Lyric to "La Mer" by CHARLES TRENET

TRUMPET

THE BLUE ROOM

TRUMPET

Words by LORENZ HART
Music by RICHARD RODGERS

BLUE SKIES

TRUMPET

Words and Music by
IRVING BERLIN

BLUESETTE

TRUMPET

Words by NORMAN GIMBEL
Music by JEAN THIELEMANS

BODY AND SOUL

TRUMPET

Words by EDWARD HEYMAN,
ROBERT SOUR and FRANK EYTON
Music by JOHN GREEN

BUT BEAUTIFUL

TRUMPET

Words by JOHNNY BURKE
Music by JIMMY VAN HEUSEN

CAN'T HELP LOVIN' DAT MAN

TRUMPET

Lyrics by OSCAR HAMMERSTEIN II
Music by JEROME KERN

Moderately and rather freely, with a lilt

CARAVAN

TRUMPET

Words and Music by DUKE ELLINGTON,
IRVING MILLS and JUAN TIZOL

Moderately

CHARADE

TRUMPET

By HENRY MANCINI

CHEEK TO CHEEK

TRUMPET

Words and Music by
IRVING BERLIN

COME RAIN OR COME SHINE

TRUMPET

Words by JOHNNY MERCER
Music by HAROLD ARLEN

DANCING ON THE CEILING

TRUMPET

Words by LORENZ HART
Music by RICHARD RODGERS

DEARLY BELOVED

TRUMPET

Music by JEROME KERN
Words by JOHNNY MERCER

DO NOTHIN' TILL YOU HEAR FROM ME

TRUMPET

Words and Music by DUKE ELLINGTON
and BOB RUSSELL

DON'T GET AROUND MUCH ANYMORE

TRUMPET

Words and Music by DUKE ELLINGTON
and BOB RUSSELL

DREAMSVILLE

TRUMPET

By HENRY MANCINI

FALLING IN LOVE WITH LOVE

TRUMPET

Words by LORENZ HART
Music by RICHARD RODGERS

A FINE ROMANCE

TRUMPET

Words by DOROTHY FIELDS
Music by JEROME KERN

FLY ME TO THE MOON
(In Other Words)

TRUMPET

Words and Music by
BART HOWARD

Moderately

GEORGIA ON MY MIND

Words by STUART GORRELL
Music by HOAGY CARMICHAEL

TRUMPET

HERE'S THAT RAINY DAY

TRUMPET

Words by JOHNNY BURKE
Music by JIMMY VAN HEUSEN

HERE'S TO LIFE

TRUMPET

Music by ARTIE BUTLER
Lyrics by PHYLLIS MOLINARY

HONEYSUCKLE ROSE

TRUMPET

Words by ANDY RAZAF
Music by THOMAS "FATS" WALLER

HOW DEEP IS THE OCEAN

(How High Is the Sky)

TRUMPET

Words and Music by
IRVING BERLIN

HOW INSENSITIVE
(Insensatez)

TRUMPET

Music by ANTONIO CARLOS JOBIM
Original Words by VINICIUS DE MORAES
English Words by NORMAN GIMBEL

Medium Bossa Nova

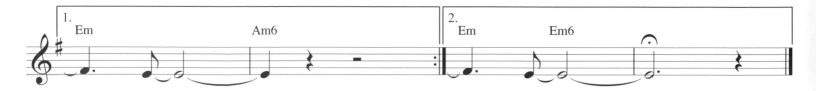

I CAN'T GET STARTED

TRUMPET

Words by IRA GERSHWIN
Music by VERNON DUKE

I COULD WRITE A BOOK

TRUMPET

Words by LORENZ HART
Music by RICHARD RODGERS

I GOT IT BAD AND THAT AIN'T GOOD

TRUMPET

Words by PAUL FRANCIS WEBSTER
Music by DUKE ELLINGTON

I'LL REMEMBER APRIL

TRUMPET

Words and Music by PAT JOHNSTON,
DON RAYE AND GENE DE PAUL

I'M BEGINNING TO SEE THE LIGHT

TRUMPET

Words and Music by DON GEORGE, JOHNNY HODGES,
DUKE ELLINGTON and HARRY JAMES

Medium Bounce

I'VE GOT THE WORLD ON A STRING

TRUMPET

Words by TED KOEHLER
Music by HAROLD ARLEN

IF I WERE A BELL

TRUMPET

By FRANK LOESSER

IMAGINATION

TRUMPET

Words by JOHNNY BURKE
Music by JIMMY VAN HEUSEN

Slowly, with a lilt

IN A SENTIMEMTAL MOOD

TRUMPET

By DUKE ELLINGTON

IN THE WEE SMALL HOURS OF THE MORNING

TRUMPET

Words by BOB HILLIARD
Music by DAVID MANN

INDIANA
(Back Home Again in Indiana)

Words by BALLARD MacDONALD
Music by JAMES F. HANLEY

TRUMPET

Moderately, with a lilt

ISN'T IT ROMANTIC?

TRUMPET

Words by LORENZ HART
Music by RICHARD RODGERS

IT COULD HAPPEN TO YOU

TRUMPET

Words by JOHNNY BURKE
Music by JAMES VAN HEUSEN

IT DON'T MEAN A THING
(If It Ain't Got That Swing)

TRUMPET

Words and Music by DUKE ELLINGTON
and IRVING MILLS

Fast Swing

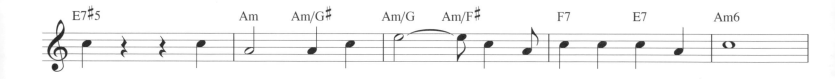

IT MIGHT AS WELL BE SPRING

Lyrics by OSCAR HAMMERSTEIN II
Music by RICHARD RODGERS

TRUMPET

THE LADY IS A TRAMP

TRUMPET

Words by LORENZ HART
Music by RICHARD RODGERS

LAZY RIVER

TRUMPET

Words and Music by HOAGY CARMICHAEL
and SIDNEY ARODIN

LET THERE BE LOVE

TRUMPET

Lyric by IAN GRANT
Music by LIONEL RAND

Moderately

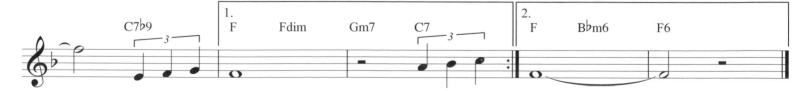

LIKE SOMEONE IN LOVE

TRUMPET

Words by JOHNNY BURKE
Music by JIMMY VAN HEUSEN

LITTLE GIRL BLUE

TRUMPET

Words by LORENZ HART
Music by RICHARD RODGERS

LONG AGO (AND FAR AWAY)

Trumpet

Words by IRA GERSHWIN
Music by JEROME KERN

LOVER, COME BACK TO ME

TRUMPET

Lyrics by OSCAR HAMMERSTEIN II
Music by SIGMUND ROMBERG

Moderately

LULLABY OF BIRDLAND

TRUMPET

Words by GEORGE DAVID WEISS
Music by GEORGE SHEARING

LULLABY OF THE LEAVES

TRUMPET

Words by JOE YOUNG
Music by BERNICE PETKERE

MANHATTAN

TRUMPET

Words by LORENZ HART
Music by RICHARD RODGERS

MEDITATION
(Meditação)

TRUMPET

Music by ANTONIO CARLOS JOBIM
Original Words by NEWTON MENDONÇA
English Words by NORMAN GIMBEL

Medium Bossa Nova

MIDNIGHT SUN

TRUMPET

Words and Music by LIONEL HAMPTON,
SONNY BURKE and JOHNNY MERCER

MISTY

TRUMPET

Music by ERROLL GARNER

MOOD INDIGO

TRUMPET

Words and Music by DUKE ELLINGTON,
IRVING MILLS and ALBANY BIGARD

MOONLIGHT IN VERMONT

TRUMPET

Words by JOHN BLACKBURN
Music by KARL SUESSDORF

MORE THAN YOU KNOW

TRUMPET

Words by WILLIAM ROSE and EDWARD ELISCU
Music by VINCENT YOUMANS

MY HEART STOOD STILL

TRUMPET

Words by LORENZ HART
Music by RICHARD RODGERS

MY OLD FLAME

TRUMPET

Words and Music by ARTHUR JOHNSTON
and SAM COSLOW

MY ONE AND ONLY LOVE

TRUMPET

Words by ROBERT MELLIN
Music by GUY WOOD

MY ROMANCE

TRUMPET

Words by LORENZ HART
Music by RICHARD RODGERS

MY SHIP

TRUMPET

Words by IRA GERSHWIN
Music by KURT WEILL

THE NEARNESS OF YOU

TRUMPET

Words by NED WASHINGTON
Music by HOAGY CARMICHAEL

A NIGHT IN TUNISIA

TRUMPET

By JOHN "DIZZY" GILLESPIE
and FRANK PAPARELLI

Moderately fast Swing

ON GREEN DOLPHIN STREET

TRUMPET

Lyrics by NED WASHINGTON
Music by BRONISLAU KAPER

ONE NOTE SAMBA
(Samba de uma nota so)

TRUMPET

Original Lyrics by NEWTON MENDONÇA
English Lyrics by ANTONIO CARLOS JOBIM
Music by ANTONIO CARLOS JOBIM

Medium Bossa Nova

PICK YOURSELF UP

TRUMPET

Words by DOROTHY FIELDS
Music by JEROME KERN

POLKA DOTS AND MOONBEAMS

TRUMPET

Words by JOHNNY BURKE
Music by JIMMY VAN HEUSEN

QUIET NIGHTS OF QUIET STARS
(Corcovado)

TRUMPET

English Words by GENE LEES
Original Words and Music by ANTONIO CARLOS JOBIM

Medium Bossa Nova

SATIN DOLL

TRUMPET

By DUKE ELLINGTON

SKYLARK

TRUMPET

Words by JOHNNY MERCER
Music by HOAGY CARMICHAEL

Moderate Swing

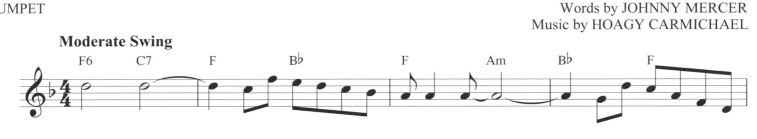

SO NICE
(Summer Samba)

TRUMPET

Original Words and Music by MARCOS VALLE
and PAULO SERGIO VALLE
English Words by NORMAN GIMBEL

Medium Bossa Nova

SOPHISTICATED LADY

TRUMPET

Words and Music by DUKE ELLINGTON,
IRVING MILLS and MITCHELL PARISH

SPEAK LOW

TRUMPET

Words by OGDEN NASH
Music by KURT WEILL

STELLA BY STARLIGHT

TRUMPET

Words by NED WASHINGTON
Music by VICTOR YOUNG

STOMPIN' AT THE SAVOY

TRUMPET

By BENNY GOODMAN,
EDGAR SAMPSON and CHICK WEBB

Bright Swing

STORMY WEATHER
(Keeps Rainin' All the Time)

TRUMPET

Lyric by TED KOEHLER
Music by HAROLD ARLEN

A SUNDAY KIND OF LOVE

TRUMPET

Words and Music by LOUIS PRIMA, ANITA NYE LEONARD,
STANLEY RHODES and BARBARA BELLE

TANGERINE

TRUMPET

Words by JOHNNY MERCER
Music by VICTOR SCHERTZINGER

THERE'S A SMALL HOTEL

TRUMPET

Words by LORENZ HART
Music by RICHARD RODGERS

THESE FOOLISH THINGS (REMIND ME OF YOU)

TRUMPET

Words by HOLT MARVELL
Music by JACK STRACHEY

THE THINGS WE DID LAST SUMMER

TRUMPET

Words by SAMMY CAHN
Music by JULE STYNE

This Can't Be Love

TRUMPET

Words by LORENZ HART
Music by RICHARD RODGERS

THOU SWELL

TRUMPET

Words by LORENZ HART
Music by RICHARD RODGERS

UNFORGETTABLE

TRUMPET

Words and Music by
IRVING GORDON

THE VERY THOUGHT OF YOU

TRUMPET

Words and Music by
RAY NOBLE

With a slow, easy Swing

WATCH WHAT HAPPENS

Music by MICHEL LEGRAND
Original French Text by JACQUES DEMY
English Lyrics by NORMAN GIMBEL

TRUMPET

WAVE

TRUMPET

Words and Music by
ANTONIO CARLOS JOBIM

Medium Bossa Nova

THE WAY YOU LOOK TONIGHT

TRUMPET

Words by DOROTHY FIELDS
Music by JEROME KERN

WHAT'LL I DO

TRUMPET

Words and Music by
IRVING BERLIN

WILLOW WEEP FOR ME

TRUMPET

Words and Music by
ANN RONELL

WITCHCRAFT

TRUMPET

Music by CY COLEMAN
Lyrics by CAROLYN LEIGH

Moderately

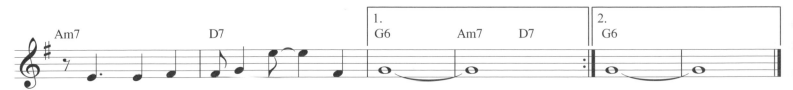

Yesterdays

TRUMPET

Words by OTTO HARBACH
Music by JEROME KERN

YOU ARE TOO BEAUTIFUL

TRUMPET

Words by LORENZ HART
Music by RICHARD RODGERS

YOU BROUGHT A NEW KIND OF LOVE TO ME

TRUMPET

Words and Music by SAMMY FAIN,
IRVING KAHAL and PIERRE NORMAN

Medium Swing

YOU DON'T KNOW WHAT LOVE IS

TRUMPET

Words and Music by DON RAYE
and GENE DePAUL